The Least of Us

How Your Imposter Syndrome Points You to Your Greatest Power

Alani Bankhead

ISBN (Paperback): 979-8-9886154-3-9
ISBN (eBook): 979-8-9886154-2-2

Dedication

To the Megans and Viveks of the world.

I was so scared when I was in your shoes. So doubtful of my value, my capabilities, and my worthiness. I now know that fear was a lie. I hope this book gives you a shortcut to arriving at the place of absolute Truth – that you have a mighty purpose, that you were built with all the tools and skills needed to do the job, and that your journey will be more successful and wilder than anything you could've ever imagined. If you only have the courage to trust.

Acknowledgments

God: you have a wicked sense of humor. Thank you for putting up with all my whining, fighting, and griping as you patiently guided me. To Lyle: thank you for the love and generosity that gave me the space to grow into my potential. Every time you've shown support for my work when I worried about its worthiness, God poked me in the ribs and reminded me that you are the earthly embodiment of what unconditional love looks like. To Amada: for always being my hype woman. To Michael Baumann, Kevin Laws, Shermain Melton, the Courage to Impact Campfire crew, my amazing clients, and everyone else who guided me, encouraged me and pushed me to write this book, I am forever grateful for your kindness, generosity, and accountability.

Table of Contents

Introduction

31 "When the Son of Man comes in his glory, and all the angels with him, he will sit on his glorious throne. 32 All the nations will be gathered before him, and he will separate the people one from another as a shepherd separates the sheep from the goats. 33 He will put the sheep on his right and the goats on his left.

34 "Then the King will say to those on his right, 'Come, you who are blessed by my Father; take your inheritance, the kingdom prepared for you since the creation of the world. 35 For I was hungry and you gave me something to eat, I was thirsty and you gave me something to drink, I was a stranger and you invited me in, 36 I needed clothes and you clothed me, I was sick and you looked after me, I was in prison and you came to visit me.'

37 "Then the righteous will answer him, 'Lord, when did we see you hungry and feed you, or thirsty and give you something to drink? 38 When did we see you a stranger and invite you in, or needing clothes and clothe you? 39 When did we see you sick or in prison and go to visit you?'

[40] "The King will reply, 'Truly I tell you, whatever you did for one of *the least of these* brothers and sisters of mine, you did for me.' – Matthew 25:31-40 NIV

PART 1

Bringing Your Fish and Loaves

CHAPTER 1

The Pit

(what it feels like;
why you can't get out)

I was trying to maneuver the dust-covered Toyota Hilux as graciously as possible over the numerous speed bumps on the way into the war zone. Although I learned how to operate a stick shift years prior, I had never consistently driven one. My poor 'terp–the affectionate nickname the military community has given our language interpreters–so graciously biting his tongue in the passenger's seat as my driving slowly compressed his spine.

As a counterintelligence operative running informants in the Middle East, my job was to obtain intelligence from people who knew the whereabouts of Al Qaeda's most senior leaders. Some of them were terrorists themselves who had killed Americans before. Part of our work involves seeking new streams of intelligence. And some weeks before, I'd found an opportunity through the equivalent of a 911 call log. An Iraqi had reported information on a pending suicide vest (SVEST) attack. I had presented the raw intelligence to my boss and told him I wanted to meet with this source. My 'terp–one of the most decorated and respected special operations linguists in the history of the Iraq campaign, his accolades too classified to discuss in this book–was in agreement with me.

My boss shot me down.

Um, what? I had an amazing lead that could supply us with new threads of intelligence, and he was telling me "no"? Why? My 'terp and I left the plywood palace that was my boss's office dejected. After a couple of minutes of silence, my linguist uttered the truth that hung in the air. A truth I was presently rationalizing in my mind:

"It's because you're a woman."

I simultaneously deep sighed and acknowledged his statement with a nod.

And so, weeks later when we received a second lead on this same stream of intelligence, my 'terp and I didn't need to say anything. One look and we were in agreement. We just went. As our bodies jolted uncomfortably over another speed bump, I knew this day was going one of two ways: I was either going to get the intelligence we needed to save lives, or I was getting sent home. The only thing more uncomfortable than the drive off base was what was the imposter syndrome raging in my head:

What if I was wrong?
What if the lead was an ambush?
Who am I to break the rules?
Maybe my boss really knew better and the nagging question about sexism was all in my head.

After months of ingesting the best counterintelligence training the world have to offer and learning how to balance risk and reward, it was a chance my intuition was telling me to take.

Seventy percent of all humans experience Imposter Syndrome. This dates back to research first conducted in the 1970s. The typical encounter involves the life-sucking experience of having that voice in your head second guess you every minute of every day. Even now, the voice rages in my own head:

"Who do you think you are?"
"Who would pay attention to you?"
"You're going to pour your soul into this thing, and no one will care. See…I told you…

…You. Do. Not. Matter."

But twenty years into this wild ride of spy and terrorist hunting, being the lead bodyguard to a top Pentagon official leading a team of bodyguards, overseeing counterintelligence operations for over 200 Air Force units worldwide, and organizing large-scale anti-child sex exploitation operations in the Pacific, I know better now. I know that when my old friend the imposter shows up, that I don't need to be scared. When that hopelessness that marks our inner imposter starts to take over my whole body and makes me want to throw up, I smirk now. Because I've felt this feeling many times before.

It means God is about to do something. And it is in this precise feeling of complete and utter weakness that I know I am exactly where I need to be. Because we serve a God who is in the business of transforming the weakest of things into the most powerful.

Yes, this book is spiritual. Yes, I talk about God and my experience with God. The Western world has placed more value on intellect (strength) than spirituality (weakness). And spiritual warfare has led many to reject their original spiritual practices or caused an outright allergy to develop. As someone who left the church for ten years due to all sorts of spiritual injury, I get it. But part of why your imposter syndrome is so loud is because you have ignored and put aside this part of yourself.

In this book, I share my own journey to harnessing my inner imposter. As a Christian, I am so grateful to Jesus for what He did for me on the cross. I am also a cusser who has willfully done plenty of sinning and unbiblical things in my lifetime. Each person's journey is unique and won't look like mine, because mine is mine and yours is yours. What is important is for you to understand how the divine created *you*.

Uniquely.
With purpose.
Mighty.
Loving.
You.

This I know to be True.* [You will notice that sometimes I capitalize the word "true." "Truth" – with a capital 'T' denotes an absolute Truth for me. Whereas "truth" – all lowercase – denotes a belief manufactured by humans or even yourself which hasn't definitely been considered and/or proven. As you read through this book and consider your mind's operating system, I encourage you to interrogate your beliefs until you arrive at a place that is a definitive Truth for you.]

I invite you to use this book as a tool. Not only will you learn the individual steps I have used with countless women and men to help them overcome their inner imposter, but–if you are open to it–you can use it as a tool to truly understand the unique ways in which you were built to solve big problems. To brightly shine your light into the darkest of spaces, to serve the vulnerable, and create ripples in the spiritual world you won't know about until you get to heaven.

If you call yourself a Christian, this tool will help you dismantle the one-size-fits-all framework you've been given that is causing you all sorts of confusion. We'll burn it all down and start rebuilding your foundation with the cornerstone being a spirituality practice rooted in understanding how you were created to interact with the Divine and filtered through the truth of the Bible. And if you're rumbling with your spirituality, start with acknowledging the soul inhabiting your body. The one that connects with a song, a book, or a movie in such powerful ways, it cannot be denied. As the art moves through you, you subconsciously find yourself wondering how you could connect so deeply with a composer or director you've never met. How you feel deeply seen and understood.

By connecting your physical world with your spiritual world and understanding how God created you to uniquely interact with Him, you will begin to plainly see how you need to move forward. Because you are not insignificant.

Welcome to the ranks of The Least of Us. The weakest army to ever exist, which God is using to heal the world.

CHAPTER 2

What is "Imposter Syndrome"?

The inner imposter. That sneaky voice that tells you you're not good enough. It whispers, "Who do you think you are?" the moment you experience one moment of inspiration as to what your next courageous calling is. It can be loud and vicious like poor, possessed Regan from "The Exorcist" or more quiet and insidious like Mike Meyers from the "Halloween" franchise. It tells you you're not qualified, don't have enough credentials, and lack the education. That you're too fat, skinny, brown, short, and tall. It points at your weaknesses as proof that you're not capable and loves to reminisce about past times you tried and failed miserably. What makes you think this time will be any different?

The accompanying feelings in your body include dread. That nasty pit in your stomach that makes you want to throw up. Or maybe your shoulders tense without you realizing it. Clammy palms and nervous ticks start. You're almost subconsciously looking for the exit or a hole to crawl into and die. Anything to make this feeling go away. It's a natural response to the chemicals being dumped into our bodies as a result of the thoughts. Cortisol and

Adrenaline flood your bloodstream, and your body involuntarily goes into a fight-flight-fawn response. All responses are refined by millions of years of evolution. Except, the fear you're experiencing from God's calling on your life isn't a result of being chased by a saber-toothed tiger. But I imagine it felt much the same back in the day for our prehistoric brothers and sisters.

The resulting behavior is avoidance. And while you may not be able to actually avoid that project at the office, you find yourself looking for any and every excuse to suddenly work on your taxes. Or the other favorites: scrolling through social media, binge-watching streaming services, reaching for that bag of greasy, delicious chips, or maybe even an adult beverage.

I get it. It's a super hard place to be. I know because I was there for the better part of the first twelve years of my career. I'm a career military officer and special agent. I have almost twenty years and, as of the writing of this book, am serving as a Lieutenant Colonel in the Air Force. I'm also a Supervisory Special Agent. You already heard a little bit about my time working in human intelligence operations for special operations in Iraq. I have also hunted spies in Asia and led worldwide counterintelligence efforts for over 200 units to protect our most classified technologies and plans. I have commanded units in and out of the Middle East. My breadth of experience as an investigator helped me find my passion in protecting the most vulnerable: children. I became a technology-facilitated child sex crimes expert and have facilitated the arrest of hundreds of child sex abusers on multiple continents through undercover operations. I was the senior bodyguard–officially titled the "Personal Security Adviser"–in charge of a team of advisers–known as "Personal Security Officers"–for one of the Pentagon's top officials.

While most people will hear or see such a resume and comment on how impressive it is, what most people don't realize is that I was scared almost the entire time.

Scared that I wasn't qualified for any of the jobs and promotions.
Scared that someone was making a grave mistake.
Scared that I would be found out as someone unworthy of the task.
Terror-stricken by the impending embarrassment

All markers, I later learned, of a concept known as "Imposter Syndrome."

Imposter Syndrome was born in the late 1970s when Dr. Pauline Clance and Dr. Suzanne Imes published a paper called "The Imposter Phenomenon in High Achieving Women: Dynamics & Therapeutic Intervention" in the Journal of Psychotherapy: Theory, Research, & Practice. They surveyed one hundred women. A third had been involved in psychotherapy sessions and the remaining two-thirds were women from lectures and therapy groups. All of them had been recognized for their professional excellence. Drs. Clance and Imes defined the imposter phenomenon as "an internal experience of intellectual phoniness" and found approximately 70% of study participants suffered from it.

More research has been done over the years, and it's been discovered that it doesn't only affect high-achieving women but men as well. Some common behaviors and thoughts experienced by individuals experiencing imposter syndrome include:

- Dismissing positive feedback and praise.
- Inability to celebrate themselves.
- Excessive worry and anxiety which creates a perpetual cycle of self-doubt.
- Fear that you'll be found out as an imposter or undeserving of promotions, titles, and/or awards.
- The belief their colleague and supervisors overestimate them.
- Not asking for raises or increased compensation.

- Over-preparing and overworking.
- Perfectionism
- Burnout
- Sabotaging your own success.

Sound familiar?

What I have found hardest about working in this field is that the imposter convinces my clients that they must keep these fears a secret. After all, the ultimate fear is that you'll be found out which keeps people from talking about it which keeps people stuck. Stuck in a perpetual cycle of self-loathing and fear you can't break out of no matter how hard you try. It causes you to question your sanity after a while. You're capable of and have achieved so much. Why can't you solve this issue?

It's because you can't "to-do" list or achieve your way to the solution. So then how do you rid your life of this energy and joy-sucker?

The journey starts with me affirming to you that you are not alone in this struggle. Even if you don't believe the statistics, I have worked with and helped hundreds of individuals who suffer from imposter syndrome. If you're willing to think outside the box and be open to new experiences, you can overcome your imposter too. It will require you to carefully examine your thought structures and burn some to the ground so that new structures may be built that better serve you.

Let's play.

CHAPTER 3

Foundational Beliefs

Every incredible human who approaches me has arrived at the end of their rope with their Imposter Syndrome. They are heart-centered, high-achievers who want to save the world. (Aside: If you're the type to read the previous sentence and think, "I'm not a leader. I am not capable of saving the world," then your inner imposter runs so deeply, it's even infected your perspective on self-leadership. If this is you, let's really go back to basics and agree that you are simply a person who is trying to be a good human.) They are exhausted and burned out from the cycle of putting their best work forward, their professional craft honed to perfection. Many may have awards on their shelves, money in the bank, or titles, but they don't feel fulfilled or happy. "Isn't this what I've worked so hard for so many years? Why don't I feel better?" they ask me. They don't even necessarily want the recognition, although the recognition has been the fuel that has kept them going. They want to feel satisfied and fulfilled. They want peace and joy in their work. They often cite God's word and how they are obedient to it:

"Do nothing out of selfish ambition or vain conceit. Rather, in humility, value others above yourselves, not looking to your own interests but each of you to the interests of the others." Philippians 2:3-4 NIV

"Greater love has no one than this: to lay down one's life for one's friends." John 15:13 NIV

They lament the life of joy and abundance God promises feels unattainable. Hadn't they done all the things they should've done?

Or if you're early in your career, the thought may go something like, "There is so much I want to do in the world, but I just don't see how I can get there." You're doing everything in your power to be part of the team and show that you can make a difference. Selfless service is a pillar of your professional ethic, but you may be resentful and tired after years of no one else reciprocating. When you talk to God or yourself, you think things like, "We're called to be selfless, so why am I so exhausted? Shouldn't I feel energized? I must be doing it wrong." Or you may have a grand plan for how you think things should be done, to tackle a major issue facing the world today or, on a smaller scale, a mission at work. "I can clearly see how we need to move forward. Why does no one else see it?" Over time, it makes you doubt if you actually do know.

And as I hear these amazing clients pour their vinegar out, I listen with a sympathetic ear. I've been there too. After the glorious word vomit, they'll always apologize and ask if what they said makes sense. It makes perfect sense. Then I tell them something they've never heard or thought of before:

You're frustrated because you don't know who you actually are.

For the high-achiever, this seems ridiculous at first. I remind them of Albert Einstein's definition of insanity. "Doing the same thing over and over expecting different results." Their old mindset has helped them achieve so much, but what they are seeking lays outside of this framework. The process of coaching, first and foremost operates on the premise that the client has all the answers they seek tucked into their DNA. As a coach, my job is to help them excavate these solutions through asking probing questions. These questions help us examine these mindset structures, identifying which beliefs truly serve or don't serve you, then choosing new beliefs to replace old ones. In my particular practice, we filter each of these beliefs through the word of God. And the truth is, my clients may know God's word, but for the most part they have ingested it via someone else's interpretation. A big reason why they are out of alignment is because they continue to hold onto beliefs that do not align with how God created them to interact with Him. Uniquely. There is no cookie-cutter spirituality. We were mostly raised understanding specific faith practices and interpretations. Lutheran, Baptist, Non-denominational, Episcopalian, Catholic, etc. If you're like me, you grew up sort of thinking they were basically the same thing. Or like some clients I've had, you were taught that other denominations were wrong. The Southern Baptists love raising their hands, dancing in the church aisles, and speaking in tongues. I've attended churches in Latin America where one service goes on for upwards of five hours. Whereas my non-denominational brothers and sisters, sit and stand stoically. Service is done exactly one hour after it starts, and not a minute later. A slight raise of the eyebrows when a visitor uplifts their hands towards the ceiling. What if we let all of those beliefs and judgments go? Let's start with the basic understanding that we all serve the same God.

And there are also different theological orientations:

- Calvinism
- Arminianism
- Molinism
- Reformed Theology
- Etc

Each with very specific interpretations of the Bible and many very vocal loyalists to accompany them. Your eyes may be glazing over, but I beg your leave to geek out on theology for just a minute longer. And it's important in helping you unearth your own True beliefs.

I walk my clients through an exercise where we discuss what they think is right. To keep it simple, I stick with the two main theological orientations of the day to introduce them to these concepts: Calvinism and Arminianism. These two themes seek to understand the relationship between man's sovereignty and man's responsibility in the matter of salvation and life.

Calvinists generally believe that there is only one plan for their lives pre-ordained by God before the world was ever created. God knows what will happen every second of their lives because he is sovereign over that plan. He even knows who will come to accept Jesus. He created it, after all! Inherently, this interpretation focuses on God's sovereignty and rejects our ability to have free will. For many people, this is very comforting. Particularly when you couple it with the beliefs that:

- God is working all things–even the "bad" ones–for our good and His glory. (Rom 8:28)
- Because of the sacrifice of Jesus on the cross, we cannot lose. (Rev 20:10)

You can't screw up God's plan for your life. Even if you willfully sin. Look at David. That guy has sex with another man's wife and then sends the poor husband to the front lines to die just to hide his transgressions and sin (2 Sam 11). And he is still one of God's favorites (Acts 13:22)! Then of course, there's the age-old story of Joseph whose brothers sold him into slavery as a result of their jealousy that he was their father's favorite (Gen 37: 18-36). Those actions put him in a position where he could eventually be the number two ruler in the land and save a country from famine (Gen 41). To be clear, we know God hates sin. But if the concept that God can work through even our darkest and most intentional deeds, brings relief or if reading this resonates, you're likely in the Calvinist camp.

Arminians conversely believe that God loves us so much, He gave us free will to make the choice on how to live our lives. The cornerstone issue around the Calvinism vs. Arminianism debate centers around salvation. Does God pre-decide who will be saved? Or does He give us the choice to decide for ourselves? But it extends beyond this initial choice into how we live our lives. And no matter what that decision is, God is sovereign over every single outcome. I like to refer to Arminianism as "alternate wormhole theory." Imagine each decision leads to a different universe, and God knows and is sovereign over each of those. Much like the multiverse that is so popular in the Marvel Universe. Or like the old TV show "Quantum Leap" where the character leapt from universe to universe helping people make different choices that altered their lives and world course forever. Arminians believe very strongly in God's love for us. He is our Father. And doesn't a parent want a child to fully express their amazing, unique selves as they grow and learn?

If you're a bit more in the Arminian camp, I then point you to Genesis. If God created the universe and everything in it and we are created in His image (Genesis 1), wouldn't that make you a creator too? Whenever I see a funny animal like giraffes, with their long necks or dogs with their wagging tails, I will often imagine God sitting around Eden creating the first of every animal. Maybe God's thought process went something like this:

> "I'm going to create an animal that will become the companion for humans. They will all have cute faces. I like floppy ears. And I'm going to add a long furry tail. It'll move the tail with glee anytime their person arrives in their presence. Even if the human left the residence but came back five minutes later, it will uncontrollably move with the same level of enthusiasm as if that human were gone for hours. I will call it 'a wag.' They will have the ability to dream, and those dreams will often involve chasing chickens."

I often imagine God had so much fun when He created creation. Rainbows, lush landscapes, vast cerulean oceans.

If you tend to lean on the Arminian side, then that means God also created you to choose what to believe and how to live your life. To create universes…*universes*.

One of my favorite parts of this debate is the Truth that both concepts are Biblically correct. It seems illogical since they are at opposite ends of the intellectual spectrum, but it's true. If you're skeptical, as I once was, decide for yourself. Here are some references:

Calvinism

> "No one can come to me <u>unless the Father who sent me draws him</u>. And I will raise him up on the last day." John 6:44

"He predestined us for adoption as sons through Jesus Christ, according to the purpose of his will." Eph 1:5

"So then it depends not on human will or exertion, but on God, who has mercy." Rom 9:16

"You stiff-necked people, uncircumcised in hearts and ears! You always resist the Holy Spirit. As your fathers did, so do you." Acts 7:51

"For those whom he foreknew he also predestined to be conformed to the image of his Son, in order that he might be firstborn among many brothers." Rom 8:29

"Even as he chose us in him before the foundation of the world, that we should be holy and blameless before him. In love." Eph 1:4

"For by grace you have been saved through faith. And this is not your own doing; it is the gift of God, not a result of works, so that no one may boast. For we are his workman-ship, created in Christ Jesus for good works, which God prepared beforehand, that we should walk in them." Eph 2:8-10

"In him we have obtained an inheritance, having been pre-destined according to the purpose of him who works all things according to the counsel of his will." Eph 1:11

"And when the Gentiles heard this, they began rejoicing and glorifying the word of the Lord, and as many as were appointed to eternal life believed." Acts 13:48

"For the Scripture says to Pharaoh, 'For this very purpose I have raised you up, that I might show my power in you, and that my name might be proclaimed in all the earth." Rom 9:17

Arminianism

"For God so loved the world, that he gave his only Son, that whoever believes in him should not perish but have eternal life." John 3:16

"The Lord is not slow to fulfill his promise as some count slowness, but is patient toward you, not wishing that any should perish, but that all should reach repentance." 2 Peter 3:9

"For 'everyone who calls on the name of the Lord will be saved.'" Rom 10:13

"Who desires all people to be saved and to come to the knowledge of the truth." 1 Tim 2:4

"In him you also, when you heard the word of truth, the gospel of your salvation, and believed in him, were sealed with the promised Holy Spirit." Eph 1:13

"But to all who did receive him, who believed in his name, he gave the right to become children of God, who were born, not of blood nor of the will of the flesh nor of the will of man, but of God." John 1:12-13

"The Spirit and the Bride say, "Come." And let the one who hears say, "Come." And let the one who is thirsty come; <u>let the one who desires</u> take the water of life without price." Rev 22:17

"If we endure, we will also reign with him; <u>if we deny him, he also will deny us</u>." 2 Tim 2:12

"For the wages of sin is death, but the <u>free gift of God</u> is eternal life in Christ Jesus our Lord." Rom 6:23

"All that the Father gives me will come to me, and <u>whoever comes to me I will never cast out</u>." John 6:37

"Behold, I stand at the door and knock. <u>If anyone hears my voice and opens the door, I will come in to him and eat with him, and he with me</u>." Rev 3:20

The fact that opposing points can be true at the same time, points us to God's mystery and reminds us that we can try to understand His ways, but that our human minds are incapable of fully comprehending. And so begins the unraveling of all that beautiful logic you've been holding on to for so long.

The key to determining what side of the spectrum you land on is peace. Which one feels more peaceful and True to you? Is there comfort in knowing that nothing you or anyone else does will get in the way of God's plan for your life? Or do you feel more peace and joy at the freedom to create your universe?

I can almost hear the steam valve in my clients' hearts releasing as they finally start to listen to what their body is telling them. This is just a strategic conversation where we examine the most basic tenets of these two frameworks. In fact, you can be a mix of both. Do you believe people can lose their salvation (Calvinism)?

Or do you believe–even if someone falls away from faith–that once they have chosen Jesus, they can never lose their salvation (Arminianism)? You can be a 2-point Calvinist or even a 3-point Arminian. It's a spectrum.

If you want to go down the rabbit hole a bit further, here's a resource adapted from Living Faith Fellowship Media.

<u>Activity: For each explanation of the TULIP framework, circle the one which most resonates with you</u>. Remembering that your connection with God is unique TO YOU, give yourself permission to release old spiritual frameworks that no longer serve you and just 'be you' in your choosing. How will you know you've chosen correctly? You'll feel a fruit of the spirit (i.e.: peace, joy, etc.).

Arminianism	Calvinism
Salvation is accomplished as man and God cooperate. Divine Grace and the human will work together for salvation to happen.	Salvation is wholly the work of the Holy Spirit. Because of his flesh and fallen state, man is unable to believe on his own and therefore needs God to decide for him.

Free Will or Human Ability	T Total Depravity	Total Inability or Total Depravity
Although humans were deeply impacted by the fall, God graciously enables each sinner to repent and believe, and He does not interfere with that freedom of choice. Each sinner possesses free will, and his eternal destiny depends on how he chooses it. Man can choose good over evil.		Because of the fall, humans are unable to believe in the gospel in their own strength. The fall causes us to be deaf to God's things, and our deceitful hearts will lead us astray. Therefore, humans cannot choose good over evil on their own.

Conditional Election	**U** Unconditional Election	**Unconditional Election**
God's choice of certain individuals unto salvation before the foundation of the world was based upon His foreseeing that they would respond to His call. He selected only those whom He knew would of themselves freely believe the gospel. Election, therefore was determined by or conditioned upon what man would do. The faith which God foresaw and upon which He based His choice was not given to the sinner by God (it was not created by the regenerating power of the Holy Spirit) but resulted solely from man's will.		God's choice of certain individuals unto salvation before the foundation of the world rested solely in His own sovereign will. His choice of particular sinners was not based on any foreseen response or obedience on their part, such as faith, repentance, etc. On the contrary, God gives faith and repentance to each individual whom He selected. These acts are the result, not the cause of God's choice. Election, therefore was not determined by or conditioned upon any virtuous quality or act foreseen in man.
Universal Redemption or General Atonement Christ's redeeming work made it possible for everyone to be saved but did not actually secure the salvation of anyone. Although Christ died for all men and for every man, only those who believe in Him are saved. His death enabled God to pardon sinners on the condition that they believe, but it did not actually put away anyone's sins.	**L** Limited Atonement	**Limited Atonement or Particular Redemption** Christ's redeeming work was intended to save the elect only and actually secured salvation for them. His death was a substitutionary endurance of the penalty of sin in the place of certain specified sinners

The Holy Spirit Can be Effectually Resisted	I Irresistible Grace	Irresistible Grace or Effectual Calling
The Spirit calls inwardly all those who are called outwardly by the gospel invitation. He does all that He can to bring every sinner to salvation. But in as much as man is free, he can successfully resist the Spirit's call. The Spirit cannot regenerate the sinner until he believes; faith (which is man's contribution) precedes and makes possible the new birth. Thus, man's free will limits the Spirit in the application of Christ's saving work.		In addition to the outward general call to salvation which is made to everyone who hears the gospel, the Holy Spirit extends to the elect a special inward call that inevitably brings them to salvation. The external call (which is made to all without distinction) can be, and often is, rejected. Whereas the internal call (which is made only to the elect) cannot be rejected; it always results in conversion. By means of this special call, the Spirit irresistibly draws sinners to Christ.
Falling from Grace	**P** Perseverance of the Saints	**Perseverance of the Saints**
Those who believe and are truly saved can lose their salvation by failing to keep up their faith. All Arminians have not agreed on this point; some have held that believers are eternally secure in Christ—that once a sinner is regenerated, he can never be lost		All who are chosen by God, redeemed by Christ, and given faith by the Spirit are eternally saved. They are kept in faith by the power of Almighty God and thus persevered to the end.

Adapted from *Living Faith Fellowship Media*, 2017

You may have already noticed a shift has occurred for you. This is a great introduction to how subsequent coaching sessions and conversations will unfold. And over time, this will be the beginning to you understanding that there are many beliefs that may have served you in the past that no longer serve you now.

I'm going to plant a seed: the internal shifts you are seeking aren't as big and scary as you think. You've been operating like a Jeep stuck in the mud. Gears going, tires slipping, as you attempt to maneuver yourself out of the muck. You really only need a few minor shifts to get you to that place where you're on a smooth ride in the comfort of your purring Volvo.

You have permission to shed all your old beliefs. In fact, you have permission to do the table sweep of rage and start over. And when we go back to the beginning, we are met with one simple Truth:

"'Teacher, which is the greatest commandment in the Law?'

Jesus replied: 'Love the Lord your God with all your heart and with all your soul and with all your mind.' This is the first and greatest commandment. And the second is like it: 'Love your neighbor as yourself.' All the Law and the Prophets hand on these two commandments." – Matthew 22:36-40 NIV

Strengthening the quality of the connection with our Father is our very top priority. This is the first seed you decide to plant. It's not about achieving, making money, or changing the world right now. It's all about the connection and re-discovering yourself and all the beautiful intricate ways in which God created you. When you start from this place, everything else will flow. It takes practice to make this shift, and all you need to focus is on making that shift for yourself today.

CHAPTER 4

Values

Julie* had come to me exhausted from dealing with her Imposter Syndrome. She had a glorious word vomit where she poured out her hopes and dreams and fears. Here's the thing about the beginning of coaching relationships: sharing your deepest thoughts with a virtual stranger can be one of the most liberating spaces. She was in psychotherapy and talked of her almost-desperation in wanting to heal the world of its deep pain. She knew she was called to it but felt so far away from walking the path. She had the education and was in the position, but something was off.

It is such a privilege to be the vehicle to hold space and be the creator of places where people can whisper their most audacious dreams. As I listened to Julie close her soliloquy with the standard, "I hope that makes sense" comment, I assured her the bridge to this sacred space of impact and meaning wasn't as long as it felt.

Our imposter pushes us to perfectionism by telling us we're never going to be good enough. And while that voice may drive us to achieve extraordinary things, we never feel that inner chasm gets filled. Any praise and accolades are met by our imposter, which tells us that we are undeserving and that people will discover our secret. And oftentimes, it's doing this in stealth mode without us being conscious of it. We wonder what's wrong with us. But you push through it and "to do" list your way to your desired outcome. But when you get to the top of the mountain of achievement, you'll look around from the perch of your hard-earned throne and feel empty.

This was how I felt at the height of my time on active duty. I had been invited out of the blue to apply for–and was eventually selected for–a position I didn't want. Being the senior bodyguard for one of the top Pentagon officials' team came with a slew of congratulations and oos and aahs from fellow co-workers and bosses. They whispered about how all the previous generals in our career field had held my position. I thought perhaps it was the beginning of a journey of grooming where the doors of opportunity would finally fling wide open and champagne would fall from the heavens. And while nothing is ever one hundred percent certain, as long as I didn't commit a felony, the chances of me at least making full bird Colonel was pretty amazing. I was on the narrow path to maybe being that top person one day. But it didn't stop my inner imposter from getting loud. It told me I was too small, young, female, and unassuming to ever be cast in such a role.

After a round of interviews, I was told I had made the top three. "Certainly," I'd silently pondered, "they'll choose one of the other candidates." My head began spinning when I got word I had been selected. "Oh my gosh, I have to do this."

God's got a funny sense of humor. He created me in that season to be in a job that literally owned me. I couldn't say 'no' even if I wanted to. I was being ordered to the Pentagon. When the reality hit me, I was surprised at the lack of excitement I'd felt. I had finally made it! All my years of hard work and sacrifice. My inner imposter had told me I needed to sacrifice everything about myself to achieve and gain acceptance. I'd always been the one volunteering to cover down in the office over the holidays, because–after all–I was the boss. "Leaders eat last, " "servant leadership," and all those things. I was also single for the first thirteen years of my career. The folks that worked for me mostly had families. I worked insane hours. A sixty-hour work week was standard but could easily ramp up to 70 to 80 hours if my caseload increased. I remember getting a stink eye from a boss once while I was living overseas. We had an impromptu operation pop up, and I'd planned on going grocery shopping that evening. I'm pretty sure I had a jar of mayo and not much else in my fridge, and we were living in a part of the world that didn't have the convenience of 24-hour restaurants, grocers, and other shopping. I'd asked for thirty minutes to run and grab some basics, and when he challenged my need for food, I had to point out that I didn't have a spouse at home running my errands or feeding me. We also lived in a more rural part of the world that didn't have the conveniences of 24/7 dining options.

But here I was. Finally on the supposed easy street with this new promotion! But this path I was on was still bumpy and windy. After the initial glee of the achievement wore off, I was surprised by a lingering question that surfaced: wasn't I supposed to be happy?

This triggered a chain of events that led me to leave active duty so I could walk the path of alignment I was meant for. And what I discovered was that it all started with foundational elements. What I believed, and who I was. I discovered I'd adopted the rest of the world's rules and values for me:

- Achieving was the focus of living.
- Success was defined by rank and power with money coming in a close third.
- I had to strip my essence away and become what others needed me to be.
- Self-sacrifice was what paved the road to acceptance.
- I would gain security the more powerful I became.

- The only values that mattered were: achievement, money, unboundaried self-sacrifice, being thin, and being white.
- Spirituality was a mechanism to keep me fearful and on the defensive, having grown up believing faith was about following a list of rules, lest you be smited.

Over time and thanks in part to my own coaching journey, I discovered myself in many ways for the first time. I was able to create awareness around these thoughts and beliefs, then I was presented with the choice to keep them or replace them. While it seems like a logical progression, receiving permission to drop these now-conscious rules was game-changing.

I replaced them with new, life-giving beliefs:

- Living was about connection: to my spirituality, to myself, and to others.
- Success was defined by freedom: having control over my schedule rather than being a slave to someone else's, choosing the projects and people I wanted to work with, following my intuition, and family. Freedom to just be me.
- I learned I couldn't pour out from an empty cup and set out to learn how to fill that cup. This included actually identifying what I needed. The truth was, I was so focused on everyone else, I wouldn't have known what to say had someone asked me what I wanted and needed. After that, I had to summon up the courage to ask for it. The first time I addressed an emotional need with my husband, I covered my face with my hoodie. But I learned that I needed to lean on my people to be able to fully show up when it was time to do the work.
- I would no longer self-sacrifice to the point of resentment. If my initial response to a request wasn't an enthusiastic "hell YES!" then it was a "no."

- I had to admit I did not provide my security – a higher power did.
- After conducting a values assessment (check out page XX for the Values Exercise!), I discovered my truest values were: connection, excellence, justice, integrity, and kindness.
- My spirituality has been distorted by well-intended family and church members. When I reviewed the Bible for myself, I discovered all the different interpretations and was able to better understand how God communicated with me. And while I am open to discussing different spiritual viewpoints, I no longer try to justify or make my spirituality acceptable to others.

And man, did things start to change.

I started connecting with others on a deeper level, and I learned an important lesson on values: not everyone has the same ones. We often try to live in a way that we exemplify all values to the best of our ability all the time. This is not sustainable. We were all created with our own unique mixture of values. I'm not saying that means the other ones don't matter, but someone else was created to embody those other values much more naturally and better than you.

As an example, I remember being asked to volunteer to do some work with the homeless. This is critically important work. Of this, I had zero doubts. But I was already giving so much of myself to the anti-child exploitation space. I could agree to do so out of obligation and because I had been taught we are *supposed* to be selfless and self-sacrificing. But over time, I learned that I'd end up resentful that I was giving away the little bit of free time I had on a mission I was not called to serve. The other thing I'd learn much later on, is by me saying "yes" meant someone else who was really meant to serve in that mission possible wasn't getting the opportunity to do so since I was taking up that slot. I learned that saying "no" to good things I wasn't called to do can be just as important as saying "yes" to the assignments meant for me.

Another way you can identify what some of your core values are is to think about what drives you most nuts about the world. For a long time, I used to get really frustrated with people who didn't hold the door open for the person coming right behind them or thank someone for holding the door for them. It takes almost zero energy to say "thank you." Eventually, I decided to make it a bit of my mission to teach these people manners. If I didn't hear a "thank you" when holding a door open for someone, I'd quip, "You're welcome!" as I flashed a syrupy smile. How passive-aggressive, right?

I knew in my body that this solution wasn't the right one, but I didn't really think there was any other option. Because the world told me not to address hard issues directly. My learned behaviors at work, school, and home were to never have a hard conversation and instead vent and gossip to co-workers and loved ones in deep judgment of that other person. Because I had been taught that no one was interested in the opinion of a young, female on…well… anything. In the world where I grew up, people who had direct conversations were labeled as rude and selfish which meant I couldn't fathom a world where I could sit down with someone and have a constructive feedback session.

The same applied to the injustice I observed in the world. Whether a powerful adult used their strength to abuse a defenseless child or if someone was wrongfully convicted, my whole body seemed to have a reaction to anything that didn't seem fair.

And while this frustration may feel very uncomfortable, our anger in the face of these values violations is your body pointing you to one of your greatest gifts to the world. Once you're aware, you are able to take action to unleash that value in the way only you were built to. For me, this meant recognizing I had kindness in spades. And as another person grabbed the door without saying a "thank you" in return, I imagined they were preoccupied thinking of some other world problem they were solving that I had zero capacity for. It made me appreciate how unique we all are, and that all those unique values combined meant we could do more to elevate humanity than we could ever possibly hope to do alone (which makes my collaboration value SING!).

I had given Lottie a homework assignment to recall powerful memories associated with each of her newly identified core values. This is a particularly important exercise because these memories serve as anchors when storms come in. She had narrowed down her list of core values to five, and the one that was the glue that held all the others together was "integrity." As we continued down memory lane, she recalled the day her parents separated. The light of truth had become a spotlight on infidelity, and she resolutely decided the pain she experienced that horrible day was going to be her reminder to live on the foundation of integrity. She had spent her whole life since committed to living with integrity so she would never inflict that kind of pain on anyone.

After reflecting her words back, I introduced the concept that this new foundation she was creating should have anabolic–or life-giving–memories at the root. While pain and fear–such as the kind imposter syndrome evoke–can lead us to survive, overcome, and achieve, they will never take us to a place of thriving, connection, and joy. I gently pointed out that Lottie's core memory associated with the value of integrity was a seed of incredible pain. As Lottie was seeking more joy in her life, the root of this new foundation she was building needed to be more hopeful. I asked her to consider a different tangible reminder of God's goodness tucked away in these values. When she'd had a few minutes to think about it, she had a bit of an a-ha moment.

She recalled another memory from that day she had forgotten about. As the unfaithful parent was walking out the door, Lottie grabbed a family photo and wrote, "I still love you" on the back and handed it to them just before they left the residence. Immediately, Lottie's body language completely softened, and the micro-lines of stress on her forehead relaxed. She visibly became emotional as she sat with the memory. Her eyes lit up as she explained that, despite whatever terrible act her parent had inflicted on the family, her entire being was telling her that everyone was worthy of their humanity. After a minute of reflection, we continued to unpack her thought process in scribbling the note. Through this exercise, Lottie broke through the fog to a moment of clarity. She had not only illuminated a core value and anchoring memory, but Lottie had also uncovered what her life purpose was: to rid the world of loneliness.

She now instinctively knew that every person she encountered would never feel alone again. This was the core seed from which everything else would grow. And fertilized with her other core values of connection, community, spirituality, and trust, Lottie's eyes were opened to the foundational elements of the beautiful universe she was about to create.

You may be wondering what core values have to do with crushing your Imposter Syndrome. And you may have even had a variation of the following thoughts:

- "I came here for solutions. A values assessment is not the type of tool I need."
- "I already know what my values are."
- "This is kind of dumb."

If any of the following applies to you, then you are in the right place!

Doing the work of understanding your basic values isn't something that is taught in most homes or schools. You may shrug off the concept because you think you know what your values are. But if you are suffering from an inner imposter, it's because you actually don't. And in fact, the imposter's voice is usually a core value that you've ignored or suppressed for so long that it's gotten louder and uglier overtime trying to get your attention. If you are reading this book, that means you are a high achiever who is very intelligent. It also means you have reached your wit's end on how to overcome your Imposter Syndrome. You have tried every tool known to man, but you still find yourself feeling less than others. So how well is that beautiful logic working to get you what you want?

One hundred percent of my clients have been surprised by the results of their values assessment exercise. And the ten minutes they take to complete the exercise are the first step they take in adopting a new operating system for their minds. Which means burning your existing mindset to the ground.

Burn, baby, burn.

CHAPTER 5

Uncovering Your Imposter Voice

By now, you've identified what your core values are and how well you've been living them day-to-day. If there is a large disparity between the two numbers, it means your imposter voice will be extra loud and even more present in your life.

But I'm curious: what did you think or feel when you got your values down to the top five? Did your heart flutter a little bit? Did they jump off the page at you? Did the thought, "Oh wow! Hello, my truest self!" pop into your mind? Congratulations! You just met or were reacquainted with your truest and best self. And that deserves celebration. And now that you have remembered who you are, let's direct our attention to who you are not.

The inner imposter voice has been running subconsciously through your head for years or even decades. You've tried to beat it and have even tried to stuff it down as far as possible, so you don't have to hear it anymore. That doesn't mean it's not on constant repeat every minute of every day.

One thing I want to prime you on is the truth that the tools used in overcoming your imposter syndrome can feel counterintuitive, but I assure you if you continue with this process, you will make great strides in lessening, removing, or even using your imposter voice to your advantage. The first Truth in this process is understanding that creating awareness around the imposter syndrome's voice and message is the single most important step you can take towards being free of it. The awareness alone causes your imposter voice to become weaker. And once you are aware, you can choose a different thought.

Uncovering the thought is so important because:

THOUGHTS → FEELINGS → BEHAVIORS

Let's use modern marketing practices as a perfect example. I may see a Pizza advertisement on a random Tuesday which causes me to have *thoughts* like, "Pizza makes me so happy!" and "Oh man, that looks so good." These thoughts will lead you down a rabbit hole where you remember all the thousands of times you've eaten pizza and the pure joy (*emotion*) that it is. This will generate cues in my body including but not limited to hunger and craving. If I blindly follow these feelings, it will probably lead me to making a call (*behavior*) to my husband and declaring we will be having pizza for dinner. And my body will be anticipating the deliciousness of a bowl until my delectable pie arrives and gets consumed.

And sometimes or often after hanging up the phone, a new *thought* pops up. "I shouldn't have pizza on a weekday. That's a treat reserved for the weekends, and my unhealthy dinner goes against my wellness goals." This leads to new *emotions* in my body including **anger** at myself for letting that clever marketing sway my thoughts. "You're so weak for caving to a commercial. I can't believe you let modern-day marketing override your brilliant intellect! You're going to feel like garbage at the gym tomorrow." I will also have some **victim** thoughts – "Why can't I just control what I eat? You're going to stay fat forever." Which may lead to unhelpful _behaviors_ like skipping my workout the next morning, because…what's the point? Or may as well top it off with a chocolate brownie, since I already busted my fitness goals. And the spiral to that negative place continues to the detriment of my emotional and physical health.

We've all heard the verse about taking our thoughts captive. "We destroy arguments and every lofty opinion raised against the knowledge of God, and take every thought captive to obey Christ." 2 Cor 1-:3-5

It may seem like a goal only attainable by saints, but holding on to your mustard seed of faith that you too can change your thoughts is the root of all change. Thanks to modern science, we now have some knowledge about the capabilities of the brain to re-wire itself. This concept is known as neuroplasticity. It involves the understanding that the brain can form and reorganize synaptic connections. The more we practice this rewiring through creating awareness of our thoughts, then deciding if we want to keep or replace that thought, we'll start noticing big changes in how we move through the world.

Going back to our pizza example, I can watch the titillating commercial and have the same thought that "pizza makes me so happy!" And it does! By having awareness about how I respond to this commercial, I can recognize I'm having the thought and decide if this thought is actually serving me or not. I can recall past times when eating pizza on a weekday made me feel guilty and shameful and how I was less motivated to meet my wellness goals. I can challenge my thoughts by asking myself: "Am I the person who comfort-eats to feel better at the moment? Or am I the energetic, fun-loving, disciplined woman waiting to bust out of my unhealthy patterns and reclaim herself?" When I think about the latter version of myself, I am reminded of myself as a young professional. I was so spunky, sharp, fit, and fun. I remember the excitement I felt in my body at the idea that I had my entire life and career ahead of me and that I got to create so many amazing memories, experiences, and results in that season. But somehow over time, she had been silenced by powerful forces–including the most dominant of all: herself – that told her she was too much. That she should sit and be quiet. Over time and in an effort to escape the discomfort in my body generated by my own thoughts, I discovered food and drinks as quick fixes for the pain I felt inside. And the pounds got piled on. I felt sluggish and not like my real self. Would that pizza be delicious? Absolutely. And I will look forward to enjoying pizza Friday after a week of eating delicious, healthy, and life-giving meals. In fact, I'd enjoy the hell out of it. But today, that pizza would not honor the person I was reclaiming.

Now, the feeling in my body is different. I feel a type of peace knowing this is a hard truth, but true nonetheless. As I eat my dinner of ground turkey taco meat on a bed of garlic cauliflower rice with avocado, tomato, cucumber, and shredded cheese on top (which is seriously delicious), my body thanks me for fueling it with life-giving food. It gives me one less barrier stopping me from going to the gym the next morning.

THOUGHT → EMOTION → BEHAVIOR

I want pizza → craving → eating the unhealthy pizza →

You shouldn't have eaten that → shame and guilt → continuing unhealthy thoughts and diet patterns.

Vs.

I want pizza but will find something that is delicious AND healthy → joy → consuming a healthy meal I find really delicious and satisfying →

"Thank you for loving me enough to fuel me and not weight me down" → peace → a little happy dance that I reclaimed myself a bit more.

The same is true for your imposter syndrome voice. Although for most readers, you don't have awareness around what the thought is since it's running subconsciously, we must partner with our body to help us uncover it. Because remember, there's always a thought behind an emotion.

The imposter usually comes in the form of an "I am" statement, and there are an infinite number to choose from. And it creates that feeling of fear and dread in your body. This is where a mindfulness practice can be really helpful. You're welcome to use whatever process helps you best learn:

- Meditation – even just 5 minutes can make a big difference
- Journaling (one of my favorites)
- Art
- Mindful coloring books
- Woodworking
- Working out

During this process, the primary focus should be–bear with me–having a conversation with that feeling. I know it may sound a little woo-woo, but just go with it for a minute. Ask the feeling, why it's there. What is the core thought behind it? And I know you're probably thinking there's no stone left unturned in that beautiful overthinking brain of yours. But I assure you, there is.

Different ways of doing this include:

- Close your eyes, and imagine there are two chairs* in an empty space. Imagine your inner imposter is sitting across from you and ask it the aforementioned questions. Once you ask, stay quiet. In Interviewing 101 class for law enforcement, they often emphasize that quiet makes us uncomfortable. But silence during an interview can be a very powerful tool. In fact, instructors advise that once we ask the question, the next person who speaks actually LOSES. So I'm telling you: you're not going to lose this round. Sit quietly until your inner imposter speaks. I think you'll be surprised by what it has to say. [*This concept is most commonly known as the "Two Chair process" pioneered by psychiatrist Fritz Perls.]
- Grab your journal, and write the question at the top of the page. Again, don't try to arrive to the logical answer. Put your pen to paper and let it move, as if you were allowing your inner imposter to control the pen. If nothing is coming, that's ok! Just start writing, and the process will unlock itself
- At the gym. On the cardio machine, on an outdoor run, or while lifting weights, imagine your inner imposter is with you. What actions is it taking right now while you're working out? What do you think that says about it? Now ask it the questions and again, stay quiet to allow space for the answers to come

If you're still having a hard time arriving at an answer, that's totally ok! You're not broken, and nothing is wrong. It can be challenging to try new concepts. Reverting back to our gym analogy, it's just like your first day in the gym. You'll be clumsy and awkward as you try to figure out how everything works and moves. But with a little help, you'll be on your way in no time.

So if you're struggling, you can go back to your memory bank and recall a past memory when your "I am not good enough/ imposter syndrome" fears were prevalent. What was the situation? Who was around you? What was happening that caused the fear that you would be found out as unworthy of that title, promotion, award, or other joy? I want you to get as specific and detailed as possible to get to that place of really reliving the event. Now imagine your inner imposter is one of the characters present and have a conversation with it.

If you settle on a generalized thought like "I am not good enough," this is a great start! But it's not actually the root thought we're seeking. I want you to start to peel the onion back. Ask your imposter, WHY you aren't good enough? What is the specific trait you're lacking that makes you wonton of the blessing you have or are seeking?

Do you see your co-workers with their Master's Degrees and you with a high school diploma or Bachelor's and feel inadequate due to a lack of education? Or perhaps you recognize how brilliant your co-workers are–just naturally talented–and immediately feel you are lacking, because you couldn't come up with the ideas that they did?

In my case, I can go back to my first time in the Middle East. I was on a military base whose name and location were classified. All the buildings were made of the familiar plywood structures created by the famed Navy Construction Battalions known as the "Seabees." (Geeky military history fact: the "Seabees" name is a heterography of their namesakes "Construction Battalions." Whose initials are "CB.") I was the only female human intelligence operator in my unit on my first deployment. I was so excited to finally be in the fight to combat terrorism, but I was equally nervous. My counterparts were all white men. There's nothing wrong with this.

But seeing the same type of person in leadership positions for most of my career resulted in me having the thought that being white and Caucasian was inherently necessary to being successful. I was neither of those things. In fact, I was worse off because of how small I was and how young I looked. And since I didn't have any of those traits, the imposter thoughts that <u>I didn't matter</u> and that <u>I was too small, Hispanic, female, and young looking</u> and therefore inferior slowly and deeply took root in my psyche.

Another common thought that may initially pop up for you as you work this exercise is: "Who do you think you are?" This is standard amongst visionaries who a) don't see themselves as visionaries and b) have a creative solution pop up in their head only to have it swatted back by their inner imposter. "Who do you think you are to present this idea to your co-workers? They'll laugh you out of the room because your plan will never work." And even though there was a tiny voice of inspiration that generated this wonderful idea, it was quickly water boarded by your imposter's voice.

Again, I encourage you to peel the layers back on this thought.

- If your idea was implemented *and worked*, how would you feel about having taken action on it?
- Where did the "who do you think you are?" thought come from?
- What is it costing you to give into this thought?

Every time you arrive at an answer, continue to ask yourself "why." It will seem tedious after a while, but if you keep digging, you will have an epiphany. And it usually feels like you've hit a nerve. When I guide clients through this exercise, they go through a gamut of emotions: curiosity, annoyance, defiance, and boredom. And when they hit that nerve, they almost always experience a strong emotional reaction. The emotional floodgate can be very confusing, as clients generally feel a mixture of:

-   Surprise at the disempowering story they just unearthed.
-   Sadness or lament at how vicious and unloving that message can be.
-   Relief from finally gaining clarity.
-   Exhaustion – because it's quite a bit of work!

While there are a million imposter statements, the most frequent ones I encounter with my clients are:

-   I am not smart enough.
-   I am not educated enough.
-   I am too fat / thin.
-   I am a bad mom / spouse.
-   I am unworthy.
-   And my personal favorite…I do not matter.

Your inner imposter isn't usually limited to one. In fact, most clients have multiples. As you continue down your journey of awareness, the goal is not to arrive to the clarity as quickly as possible. But to give yourself the time and space necessary to allow these questions and thoughts to percolate and surface at the right time. One client discovered what she called a "super imposter" which she likened to a tree. And this super gremlin had branches spawning from it which represented lesser but still powerful imposter voices.

Write down your imposter "I am" statements below:

And just like that, you have taken the first and most powerful step in overcoming your Imposter Syndrome. Well done!

CHAPTER 6

Naming Your Gremlin

Before we roll into the next action step, I want to acknowledge and celebrate you for taking the very courageous step of uncovering that imposter core message. Bringing those subconscious thoughts to the surface is single-handedly *the most* important action step you can take to beating your imposter syndrome. Because now that you know what the message is, you can learn how to interrupt that thought and replace it with more empowering messages. And if you're reading this thinking that celebrating this step feels dumb or useless, I would advise you that this is also your inner imposter talking. In its extensive efforts to keep you small and stuck, it has also been telling you that you are not worthy of celebration. It says giving yourself a pat on the back doesn't achieve anything. But you are a human being. We all need and deserve to be celebrated. So take a minute to do acknowledge the powerful step you just took. No, seriously. High-five yourself. Or if you're feeling especially frisky, you can try my favorite: the parking lot happy dance.

For Step 2, we will be naming that nasty little imposter. Again, I know this may seem rather unconventional. And stop rolling your eyes at this book. How well have you been able to bust your imposter syndrome up until now? Exactly! You need to try something new.

The reason why this step is so important is because we need to continue on the journey of creating separation between you and that nasty little gremlin. [Yes, like the movie. You will notice, moving forward, that I will use this and your 'imposter' interchangeably.] And while you may have uncovered this subconscious gremlin voice, it will still feel like it's a part of you. Thankfully, it is not!

This tool was developed by the Institute of Professional Excellence in Coaching (iPEC), and it completely changed my life and the lives of my clients. They key is, you want to name your gremlin after a television, movie, book, or some other fictitious character or person whom you don't actually know. I also recommend this name be the embodiment of your gremlin. One example of someone who had three imposter voices led them to name the trio after the Kardashian sisters, Kim, Khloe, and Kourtney. Her inner saboteur was always very critical of her for not being pretty enough, and so the Kardashians personified the right amount of glamour and cattiness she felt battling within her. Another client named hers after Marlena Gru who was Gru's hyper-critical mother from the Pixar movie "Despicable Me."

You may be drawing a blank as to what that name should be. And that is ok! Sometimes it takes a few weeks for that name to bubble up to the surface. I trust that by simply asking yourself the question, the right persona will present itself to you at the right time.

Another tool that helps uncover your gremlin(s) is recovering painful past core memories and asking yourself how these memories may inform your inner imposter voice. This proved a helpful exercise for me personally. I knew my inner saboteur's core message was that I did not matter, but where did it come from?

As I searched for this answer, I reflected on my childhood. I had grown up in an imperfect but loving home. My parents had very high standards for me, but they never projected the message–whether physical, verbal, or otherwise–that I didn't matter. I was baffled for a while about where that message could have come from. And then, it came to me. A memory from my time in undergrad.

I double majored in Latin American Studies and Crime, Law, and Justice and minored in Military Studies at the Pennsylvania State University. While I had been creative in being able to double-dip credits to satisfy both degree requirements, I found myself going into my senior year realizing I still needed to take an overload of classes to graduate within four years. I was so dang poor in college that I couldn't afford to stay another semester. The Policy required that I obtain the approval of an academic advisor to take the 18 credit hours for my last two semesters. To be frank, I wasn't the greatest student in college. I had gone into that last year with barely a 3.0 GPA. While I'd had contact with this professor in the past, I didn't have particularly strong feelings toward him either way. But I learned quickly that he certainly had some about me.

During my meeting with him, he berated me and told me I'd never amount to anything. I'd never graduate–much less with two degrees–and that I'd never commission into the United States Air Force. Needless to say, it was a tough pill to swallow. He signed the form though. And although it was really painful, that conversation also lit a fire under me.

For the next two semesters, I completely dedicated my energy to excelling academically and ended up earning a 3.96 GPA over the 36 credits while doing ROTC and working. I graduated on time. On my commissioning day when I became a second lieutenant, I scanned my two undergraduate degrees, my commissioning certificate, and my senior year transcript and sent him an email thanking him for everything he did for me. He was the only academic advisor not present at my commissioning.

I did my "gremlin naming" exercise around 14 years after this interaction, and the memory still felt really raw. Over the years, it would occasionally come to mind. But I always found it odd that that memory would pop into my head at the most random times. What I know now is that my inner imposter was born on that day. And when I distilled the entire interaction, the core message I received from him was that I did not matter and never would.

One of the benefits of Imposter syndrome is that it can really spur you to prove that voice wrong or at least work really hard so you can live to see another professional day. Hence why perfectionism and burn out are symptoms of imposter syndrome. I shared how that interaction caused me to become hyper-focused on my studies. What I didn't realize until I did this exercise was how I had carried that interaction and voice with me into everything I did professionally after that. In every unit I arrived at after that, I was constantly doing everything possible to prove that I was value-added and indispensable. I worked excessive hours, never said 'no,' and hardly ever took holidays.

Remember how I shared my experience in "arriving" professionally when I took the Pentagon job but felt empty? It was because I had been doing everything from the root seed of memory. And that seed was rotten with defiance and even deeper still, sadness.

The "I don't matter" gremlin (THOUGHT) caused me to experience fear of rejection (FEELING) which led me to try to control the situation and overwork (BEHAVIOR). And while I had achieved professionally in very impressive ways, it was because the root thought was one rooted in fear. For probably my last few years on active duty, I knew there was another part of me ready to be unlocked. I was pushing against a glass ceiling I had no idea how to break.

My a-ha moment came when I intuitively realized I could not achieve the best version of myself when my actions were born from seeds of fear and control. This sentiment is echoed in Galatians 5:19-21.

"The acts of the flesh are obvious: sexual immorality, impurity, and debauchery; idolatry and witchcraft; hatred, **discord**, **jealousy**, fits of rage, **selfish ambition**, dissensions, factions, and envy, drunkenness, orgies, and the like. I warn you, as I did before, that those who live like this will not inherit the kingdom of God."

You may recognize this verse follows the same format as the famous "fruits of the spirit" passage in Galatians 5:22-23.

"But the fruit of the Spirit is love, joy, peace, forbearance, kindness, goodness, faithfulness, gentleness and self-control. Against such things, there is no law."

As you continue down your journey of uncovering, understanding and defeating your imposter syndrome, the fruits of the spirit are the next tool I point clients to. Since our minds will be confused and will want to go back to our old ways, we need to create and reinforce new neural pathways.

I give my clients very simple guidance: if the decision you're making invokes (FEELING) a fruit of the spirit, then they are walking in alignment with who God created them to be. And they can press on! If the client is feeling that conflict, fear, and/or the imposter's voice – the fruit of the flesh – I invite them to pause and get curious about what's going on in their body (again, the feeling) then work backward to uncover what that subconscious *thought* it.

I inherently knew that my Truth moving forward was that, in order to achieve the very best version of myself, I needed to replace this poisonous memory with the more powerful seed born of the fruits of the spirit. To do this, it starts with a simple question:

What emotion would I rather have going through life?

In my case, I desperately wanted peace and joy (FEELING). And in order to experience this in my body, what thought would I need to have? I'd have to believe that I do matter. And not just that I matter, but that have incredible value and gifts to unleash into the world. Gifts that God created me to use in service to humanity. I can continue going down this rabbit hole and get very specific about why I believe these things. My personal belief system tells me that Jesus came to beat Satan (Col 2:15) and that absolutely nothing would stand in the way of me achieving that mission (Isaiah 14:27). Not even me. Also, the enemy literally can't win (THOUGHT). Thinking through these thoughts got me to that place of peace (FEELING), and other things started bubbling up to the surface that surprised me. I suddenly had energy and wanted to create (BEHAVIOR) things to fulfill that journey.

To recap:

Step 1 – identify your gremlin voice(s).

Step 2 – name your gremlin(s).

Step 3 – begin interrogating every emotion that goes through your body. If it's a fruit of the spirit, you can proceed! If it's a fruit of the flesh, that's our invitation to pause and get curious about what's going on in our minds and hearts.

CHAPTER 7

Other energy blocks

You've identified, named, and started confronting your gremlin – the most powerful of the energy blocks. Great job! There are some other less powerful energy blocks that are also really important to address. I'm going to cover them in the order of how powerful they are.

1. Limiting belief

The limiting belief is the weakest of all the internal blocks, but it can still wreak havoc on your decision-making process and hinder your ability to really lean into your true purpose. A limiting belief is a thought or mindset you picked up along the way which you believe to be an absolute truth. Most of the time, they are subconscious beliefs. But as a reminder, awareness is the most powerful tool in your arsenal to living your most joyful life. Once you are consciously aware of a limiting belief, the solution is simply to change it.

When I was selected for bodyguard duty, it felt like my head was spinning during the transition. "How had I been selected? There's no way I'm going to be effective in this job…" As I set these thoughts on replay, my brain sought logical solutions to them. The same familiar emotions and reactions came up. My nervous system was sounding alarm bells in my head, and my old friend Dread took residence once again in the pit of my stomach. All I wanted to do was throw up as my fight or flight reaction went into full swing.

It got worse when I showed up at the school where I was to learn advanced personal security operations. On the first day of class, we introduced ourselves and shared what position we were going to. There were less than fifteen students in the class, and I was the only female.

Strike one.

In the personal security world –also known as "close protection" in other parts of the world – there is one person in charge of the team of Personal Security Officers. This person's title was "Personal Security Adviser (PSA)." This was a clear delineation that they were the responsible agent who took the bullet for the boss and accepted responsibility for any failures. As class introductions continued, I discovered I was one of three PSAs in the room.

Strike two.

My heartbeat started to quicken at the thought of all the ways I would be expected to set the example and be perfect. As the last student shared their assignment, I also realized that my protectee was the most senior of all the protectees represented in the room. In fact, the only security details more senior to mine in the hierarchy were the Secretary of Defense and the President of the United

States. This is important because chain-of-command is everything in the military. It's how we maintain good order and discipline and responsibly wield the awesome responsibility the American people have entrusted to us. If we had been at a major event with all of the most senior Pentagon officials, the Order of Precedence for the Department of Defense said only four other individuals in the entire US military establishment were more senior in position.

Strike three.

I was the most junior in rank of the two other male PSAs. Yet somehow, the smallest and most feminine person in the room was the senior security advisor out of everyone. How on earth did that happen?

I could feel the chunks rising up through my esophagus.

Remember that one of the keys of Imposter syndrome is a fear of being found out and outed as not being good enough. The key to my armor that kept me safe was never sharing my fears or vulnerabilities with anyone for fear they would out me, I'd get fired, lose my career, lose my livelihood, and end up destitute. I had no idea how I was going to resolve the mystery of how on *earth* I became a senior bodyguard and what the heck I was going to do to survive without upsetting the status quo.

During a break from classroom time, I somehow found myself in the smoke pit with another instructor. I'm not a smoker, but in the military, the smoke pits can be places where a lot of work gets done. In previous assignments, we would brainstorm the best ruses and interview themes for cases in the smoke pit. My overwhelming fear must've caused me to levitate towards it because I don't remember walking there. I only remember the words when they came tumbling out of my mouth toward my potbellied and gruff instructor.

"What the hell am I doing here? I do NOT fit the part."

I could tell the instructor was equally as surprised as I was at the words that came out of my mouth. It was a rare moment of me being vulnerable. I immediately felt relief that my dirty little secret was out but also deeply regretted saying them. Great. Now he was going to tell everyone my dirty little secret, and everyone will know without a shadow of a doubt that I don't belong there. I imagined myself getting pulled out of class that day and sent packing to my new assignment in Siberia. But just as quickly, the surprise melted away from his face as he took another long drag off his cigarette. As he exhaled the smoke, he looked at me and said, "Alani. Personal Security Operations have nothing to do with what you look like. Not your size, appearance…nothing. The work is all about how you use your brain to control your physical sur-roundings. In fact, you have an advantage your male counterparts do not. You don't look like what society thinks a bodyguard should look like which gives you the element of surprise. This job is not about making your roundhouse kick look perfect as you usher your protectee out of harm's way like in the movies. We don't care what it looks like. In fact, it'll probably look really ugly. As long as you separate your protectee from the threat, that is mission success."

And as he raised his cigarette to his lips again, he paused and muttered, "Plus, it takes the same amount of strength to pull the trigger on a gun whether you're a man or a woman. Guns are the great equalizer." He was right. My trigger finger worked just as well as the boys. In fact, I was a better shot than the majority of them.

And so I came face-to-face with a bunch of limiting beliefs that prevented me from living joyfully:

1. I am too small to be a bodyguard.
2. I am too female to be a bodyguard.
3. I am too Latina to be a bodyguard.
4. I look too young to be a bodyguard.
5. I am too physically weak to be a bodyguard.

6. The aforementioned weaknesses made me incapable of leading other bodyguards.

Cognitively, once you're aware of your limiting beliefs, all you need to do is decide if they're serving you or not. And if they are not, you can choose to replace them with a most powerful, life-giving belief. In the case of my bodyguarding duties, my instructor had presented me with new beliefs:

1. My physical appearance gives me an advantage in bodyguarding operations.
2. Other peoples' biases give me the element of surprise and make my protectee safer.
3. Security operations are about methodically controlling the space your protectee occupies.
4. I am an expert marksman.
5. My greatest strength as a leader is that I care deeply about the people and the mission.

These reframes led me down a different kind of rabbit hole. One where I was reminded of who I was and where I came from:

- I have been in war zones where I was shot at and mortared.
- I had volunteered to give my life for my country because I believe in its principles.
- My country handpicked me out of hundreds of other candidates to protect one of the most senior defense officials during a precocious time.

Slowly, I could feel my confidence coming back. I had a little bit of hope thanks to an instructor who assured me a fun-sized bodyguard could get the job done just as well or better than a full-sized one.

If you want to take it up another notch, then I invite you back to revisit your spiritual practice. What Truths can you recall to help dispel your limiting beliefs and reinforce the life-giving ones? For me, this was another iteration of 2 Cor 12:9a: "But he said to me, 'My grace is sufficient for you, for my power is made perfect in weakness.'"

What I knew to be True was that God used the weakest tools to manifest His power.

- Moses used a rod – which turned into a snake (Exo 7:8-13) and parted the Red Sea (Exo 14:16)
- David:
  - Wasn't even included in the initial panel of potential successors to the king, because his father thought he was too small and weak. He was out tending sheep! (1 Sam 16)
    - "But the Lord said to Samuel, 'Do not consider his appearance or height, for I have rejected him. The Lord does not look at the things people look at. People look at the outward appearance, but the Lord looks at the heart.'" 1 Sam 16:7
    - "Jesse had seven of his sons pass before Samuel, but Samuel said to him, 'The Lord has not chosen these. So he asked Jesse, 'Are these all the sons you have?' 'There is still the youngest,' Jesse answered. 'He is tending the sheep.'" 1 Sam 16:8
  - Defeated Goliath with stones
    - "Then Saul dressed David in his own tunic. He put a coat of armor on him and a bronze helmet on his head. David fastened on his sword over the tunic and tried walking around because he was not used to them. 'I cannot go in these,' he said to Saul, 'because I am not used to them.' So he took them

off. Then he took his staff in his hand, chose five smooth stones from the stream, put them in the pouch of his shepherd's bag and, with his sling in his hand, approached the Philistine [Goliath]." 1 Sam 17:38-40

A staff, five stones, a shepherd's bag, and a sling. The world's logic says the big fancy armor of a king is what you need to stand before a giant and be taken seriously. It is the best armor on the planet, so it'll keep you most protected. The rest of the world would've taken the armor, but David recognized that not having it made him more agile.

And down went the giant.

When it was all said and done, I had zero use of force incidents during my two years as a Personal Security Advisor at the Pentagon. I would occasionally have check-in calls with some of the instructors, and one day, one shared they'd been receiving reports of individuals with mental health issues challenging some of the teams. The would-be perpetrators saw a tall, muscular guy in a suit with an ear-piece and immediately knew they were the body-guard. And their illnesses caused them to show aggression toward the teams.

Keep in mind that, when you're on a protection mission, all you're doing is scanning for threats. Your brain never stops. And when you're met with a potential threat, you don't know what's actually going on in the other person's brain. All you know is that there is a threat, and I don't know what their intention is. And in the moment, the "why" is inconsequential. All I know is, I need to neutralize it ASAP.

And so the instructor had posited the theory that perhaps my unusual appearance directly contributed to my ability to keep my protectee safe. My "weakness" might just have been the element that drove my success.

Isn't that something?

2. Interpretations

As we move through life, we make observations of human behavior. And after a while, we get a sense that we can arrive at a conclusion about what someone meant when they said or did something. Interpretations are – by definition – the action of explaining the meaning of something. And we love to think our interpretation is right one hundred percent of the time. To understand the nuances of interpretations, we must first discuss the difference between hearing and listening.

Hearing is the physical process of perceiving sound while listening, is the process that occurs in our brain where we cognitively interpret and respond to what we heard. And all sorts of things can go awry from the time we physically hear someone say something to us to when we respond.

I use to live in Hawaii, and one thing I discovered shortly after moving there was how locals used the shaka. The shaka is more commonly known to tourists as "the hang ten", where your thumb and pinkie are extended while your three middle fingers remain curled against your palm. I learned this iconic gesture was also frequently utilized while driving. One day, I observed a vehicle trying to merge into my lane, and as I slowed a bit to allow them space, a husky Hawaiian threw up a shaka out his window signaling his gratitude. And if you let an island bus in, even the sign one the back of the bus would light up with an alternating "shaka" sign and "mahalo" meaning "thank you" in Hawaiian. Yes, y'all. Even buses show gratitude! Before long, I would make any sort of excuse to be extra polite on the road so I could experience this phenomenon again. So you can imagine my disappointment when I would show kindness to someone and got nothing. No head nod, no "thank you" mouthed via their rearview mirror…no shaka. If

I'm really honest, my immediate interpretation for the lack of gesture was because they were just plain rude. And since kindness is one of my core values, this makes me particularly allergic to anyone who I perceive as unkind. I may drive for a couple more miles stewing at what kind of a grinch wouldn't even throw a simple shaka back. It takes half a second, and it spreads so much joy. The older version of me would've settled on a concrete conclusion: this bruddah (brother) has no aloha (love).

One day, I was meeting with my church small group when the topic came up. And one friend described a similar interaction a friend of hers had while driving. Rather than identifying the other driver as being rude, she arrived at a different interpretation: "Must have carpal tunnel, no can make shaka," she had said in the local Hawaiian pigeon dialect. Carpal tunnel is a medical condition where an individual may experience frequent numbness or tingling in their fingers, especially the thumb, index, and middle fingers, which inhibits the usage of the hands. I immediately felt the frustration I'd accumulated from the highway, melt away as God served up a nice, big slice of humble pie. What if they weren't rude? What if they just couldn't physically manage the gesture?

This epiphany gave way to other alternate interpretations. What if they were:

- Distracted by an emergency situation they were rushing to get to?
- Struggling internally with a fight they'd just had and didn't even notice my kindness?
- Having a bad day and couldn't muster the joy?

I realized how unnecessarily judgmental I had been. Even if their intention was to be entitled as they drove, wouldn't I rather live in a world where grace was extended as freely to others as it had been to me?

And as I digested this thought – along with the remaining bit of my humble pie – a new feeling made its presence known: peace.

3. Assumptions

Assumptions are the next most powerful energy block. Still less powerful than a gremlin but more powerful than limiting beliefs and interpretations. An assumption is rooted in the belief that because something happened in the past, it will happen again.

"Every time I ask my kids to do the dishes, it always ends in a big fight."

"I have been praying for years that God heal my mother, but He hasn't."

Remember that THOUGHTS → EMOTIONS → BEHAVIORS. These thoughts manifest in specific ways:

"Every time I ask my kids to do the dishes, it always ends in a big fight."

-   Knowing dinner time is ending, you will again ask the kids to do the dishes
-   Your mind unconsciously goes to the same old narrative.
    o   Assumption: if I ask the kids to do dishes, there will be a fight (thought).
-   This assumption may cause you to feel a pit in your stomach as your body braces for another fight (emotion).
-   You resolve to motivate your kids to do the dishes as you start making a list of all the arguments and persuasive techniques at your disposal to get them to comply. I could

bribe them with more video game time or threaten them with being grounded.

- Before you know it, your armor is up (behavior) as you get ready to go into a battle since your assumption is that you'll end up fighting with your kids. And guess what? You do, because you walked into a conversation ready to go to war.

"I have been praying for years that God heal my mother, but He hasn't."

- You have stopped praying (behavior), because what's the point (thought)? God hasn't answered any of your other prayers.
  o Assumption: if I pray again, God will not answer me.
- The thought is churned by despair (feeling) that you are powerless to do anything to help your mom.
- Your subsequent anger (feeling) towards God over His lack of intervention causes you to distance yourself (behavior) from your spirituality.

Thankfully, there's a solution. Much like interpretations and limiting beliefs can be replaced with alternate and more life-giving ones, you can choose a different thought. When you've identified what the assumption is, it can be filtered with one powerful question:

How true is it that if you do it again, you will get the same result?

The Truth is that there is always a chance you'll get a different outcome. And when you recognize this as a possibility, all sorts of opportunities start to present themselves.

Maybe the kids won't fight you this time. And if they don't, won't all that preparation to get into the fight have been wasted energy? Rather than winding yourself up to go into battle, you could've spent that time and energy imagining how could show your appreciation for your kids (ice cream? Game night?) or even thinking up all the different ways you can utilize that time your kids are doing dishes for some much-needed "you" time.

What if you pray this time and God *does* answer your prayer? Your mother is healed! Your relationship with the divine is stronger than ever because you didn't doubt and fall away.

Interrogating your assumption gets you out of victim mode ("The kids ALWAYS make me out to be the bad guy!" and "I can't do anything to help my mom."), and it moves you to a place of empowerment and action.

What are some assumptions that drive you absolutely crazy? List them below.

1. ____

2. ____

3. ____

4. ____

PART 2

Strategies to Deal With Your Imposter

You've done the hard but important work of identifying your Imposter syndrome's core message as well as other mindset blocks which prevent you from boldly pursuing your life purpose.

Now, we'll continue peeling the layers back on your obnoxious and ever-present gremlin. This is an important progression because what most people don't understand is that your Imposter syndrome is actually a gatekeeper. And this gatekeeper protects you from experiencing pain and failure. But how does that make sense?

It's actually pretty simple.

Your life purpose is really important to you since it's the driving force of your existence. What problem were you put on earth to solve? Not sure what the answer is? There's no need to worry and panic. We'll get to identifying what your life purpose is later. What's important right now is that you understand that you have an incredible purpose and that one of your deepest fears is not accomplishing this assignment. So your brain concocted this persona that gives you all the reasons you *shouldn't* wholeheartedly pursue your life purpose to keep you safe from failing. Because if you don't take action, you can't mess up. And so you avoid disaster, criticism, and embarrassment.

Uncovering the core message is the most critical step because you can't unsee what you've seen. Now you can take action to counter it, obliterate it, or even harness it. We will explore all of those options.

CHAPTER 8

Acknowledge and Dismiss It

You'll remember from Chapter 5 that I encouraged you to have a Two Chairs conversation with your gremlin to get some initial feedback on why it was there. It was an important step for you to re-learn how to tap into the deepest part of your psyche. What you likely discovered was that it had a surprising message for you. This is obnoxious particularly for the high-achiever, because you believe you're at the top of your thinking game. But there are parts of you that have gone unexplored because you simply didn't know this territory existed. Welp, now you do. And with this awareness brings the next opportunity, to discover the hidden gems your gremlin has been protecting.

So we're going to go back to that Two Chairs exercise and invite our gremlin back to have another conversation. Again, if you're resistant to this exercise, that is completely normal. I want to remind you that your gremlin isn't as powerful now that you've uncovered it. And your gremlin is a little surprised that you actually paid attention to it rather than just dismissing it. What if your gremlin is finally feeling seen and is ready to talk? I promise this exercise will be between us, and no one will find out. You've been suffering for so long, so what do you really have to lose?

Your gremlin doesn't only have its core message on repeat. Your gremlin is—in part—a core value that you have ignored for too long. The world told you that you should value other things, and in good faith, you listened to them. Over time, one of your core values was ignored for so long that it got annoyed. Maybe it sent off a few warning signals, but you stuffed those too. Until it became a full-blown imposter voice. Perhaps it's loud and screechy or maybe it's become a sinister and menacing voice of judgment and condemnation for denying your true self.

This time, if you're comfortable, I encourage you to meditate during this conversation. Find yourself a quiet space where you can sit or lie comfortably. It's preferable to sit, but do whatever works best for you which allows you to be free from distraction and discomfort. Close your eyes, and imagine there are two chairs in an empty room. Having already identified and named your gremlin, imagine that persona is sitting in one of the chairs. Remember that it can't hurt you. As you think through the core message and how this character is representative of that message, I also want to remind you that it's not a part of you. This is one of the main reasons that we took all that time to name it. As a result, its power is diminished.

As you sit in the chair, acknowledge it. You can observe it, ask it how it's doing, express your frustration towards it…any one of a plethora of options exists. Since you're doing this in the privacy of your mind, feel free to explore whatever line of questioning pops up. When you're ready, engage your gremlin by asking it one or as many of these questions as you'd like:

- Why are you here?
- What is it you're scared of?
- What are you protecting?

- What have you been trying to tell me?

Once you ask the question, stay quiet and wait until the gremlin speaks first. This is the most important part of the process.

Even the most skeptical of clients return to the next session surprised by what the gremlin has to say. They share stories of their gremlins immediately deflating and sadly recounting all the times they had tried to alert the client to an important responsibility only to be met with being stamped out. Or their inner imposter defiantly accuses my client of not fulfilling their highest potential. As your gremlin continues to share, give it space to vent. Much like actual humans, we all need to be acknowledged and validated in our pain points and efforts. Most of the time when we're frustrated about something, we're not even really seeking solutions. We just want to know that someone sees us and cares.

Do the same with your gremlin.

Give it all the space it needs to vent. Ask the follow-up questions you would want asked if you were sitting in the chair venting to a safe person.

My clients come back reporting some fascinating conversations. They are able to get insight into their imposter syndrome, and they're able to unearth their first treasure: confirmation of what their core value (or values) is/are.

Mr. Mayor, my "I don't matter" gremlin, is the bodyguard to my value of humanity. I have always loved people and been fascinated by them. There have been over 100 billion people to walk the earth, and yet somehow each of them is unique in every way. How is that possible? I love hearing peoples' stories and reflecting their greatness back to them. I love being exposed to different perspectives and thought processes online and interacting with the framers on social media. The first thing I ask someone when I meet them is, "What's your story?" I wholeheartedly believe that every person has a unique mission they've been given in life, and they were created to be the very best at accomplishing that mission. So it makes sense that my gremlin tells me that *my* humanity is inconsequential. Because if my humanity had value, I would have the courage to put myself out there in helping to elevate other humans to the max extent possible. And this work is scary. It requires me to put myself out there exposing myself to criticism. I demand, I let others see the real me, so they can experience their humanity reflected in someone else and so they know they're not alone. I know being this example gives them the confidence to self-actualize. I could leave it at that and drag people kicking and screaming on their way up to achievement. But folks then have to white-knuckle and grit their teeth on the way there. And that's no fun. I know I was built with the tools to get them there with actual joy and to show them how to do so.

"Consider it pure joy, my brothers and sisters, whenever you face trials of many kinds, because you know that the testing of your faith produces perseverance." James 1:2-3 NIV

The methods of God's kingdom are counter-cultural to the world. Rejoicing in trials is a very advanced spiritual practice and one which you can flex well with practice. That is exactly what coaching does. It gives you safe spaces to practice flexing. As you are sent into the world to apply what you learn, you engage in a learning process where you can practice new techniques and see how they work out. Remember the fruits of the spirit vs. the fruits of the flesh. How well do your new processes serve you? The more you practice and refine your process, the quicker you'll arrive to knowing what works for you. So don't be afraid to "fail," because it's only a mechanism of learning.

I was running an anti-child exploitation operation one day where I directed at least fifty agents, intelligence analysts, and support staff. During a conversation with a co-worker, I noticed I had a lot of resentment built up towards them. The circumstances behind the buildup don't really matter. When I did the internal work of understanding why I was so frustrated, a limiting belief surfaced: "You are not allowed to show anger." The more I dug, the more I realized I had allowed myself to be conditioned to be "a good girl." Always do what you're told. Never challenge authority even if you factually know you're right. Especially, don't challenge a man; it's your job to protect their ego at your expense. Smile. If you're upset about something, stuff it down. My spiritual teaching that we should humble ourselves had been morphed by my gremlin into a message that said, "The other person is always more valuable than you are, so your opinion is always 'less than.'"

I spent years trying to silence my inner imposter using all the intellectual tools at my disposal. But all my gremlin needed sometimes was to be heard. And when I did the work of hearing him out, his power over me decreased. The same thing happens for many clients. In fact, some report back that their gremlin completely goes away. But keep in mind that people usually have multiple imposter voices. Giving voice to one may prove effective while a different tactic is preferred for another.

You can use the two-chair technique whenever you'd like to bring to light your gremlin's fears, concerns, and hopes.

If you find meditating or mindfulness to be difficult practices, again you're welcome to use any other tool which you find most resonates. You can journal the questions. Inviting the process of stream of consciousness can unlock the same process. Allowing your pen to flow without judgment and seeing what comes out will also surprise you. Yet another option is art journaling, if you're the creative type.

Before, during, and after this process, I'd also encourage you to create awareness around what's going on inside your body. Are you feeling skeptical of this process? Skepticism is a form of anger because you're making a pre-judgment as to whether the process will work or not. That's ok. Note it, and move on. When your gremlin is talking to you, does what they say to make you feel sad? Angry? Do you feel compassion toward your gremlin? These are all important clues to helping you understand what motivates your gremlin and how to overcome or harness it. It's also not necessary to fully understand what you're experiencing right now. There's nothing to resolve or achieve. The focus is on getting you a place where you accept "just existing" right now. You've probably also noticed you're moving away from the judgment you had on yourself and your gremlin. Things went from "good/bad" and "right/ wrong" to a place of less or no judgment since you're able to see a softer side of your gremlin. Give yourself time to process and listen to your intuition–and even your gremlin! This is all about you DECIDING to have a different mindset. Everything else will flow from there.

Another tool you can utilize is to simply dismiss the gremlin. As you grow deeper in your understanding and experience that your gremlin is not in fact a part of you, you will notice your relationship with it changing. Many times, giving it time to vent to you then simply dismissing it is enough to break it of its power. Any version of: "Thank you for sharing your concerns with me, but I understand my purpose and vision and can take it from here" to "I understand and appreciate that you are really trying to protect me, but your services are no longer needed" work. A simple tool but very effective.

CHAPTER 9

Harness Your Gremlin

And now, things get fun.

Imposter syndrome? Fun? YES, honey, yaaassss! *insert Z-snap* Because here's the thing:

Your gremlin points you to your superpower(s).

We previously discussed how your gremlin is an ignored value that has gone awry. And although we talked through how to give that distorted value a voice, we haven't fully discussed what that really means.

Your gremlin is the key to showing you how to unlock your greatest strengths and potential.

All this time, you've been trying to avoid your gremlin. Rationalize it away. Prove it wrong. Make. It. Go. Away.

And even though it felt scary in your mind, you now know your gremlin was merely the bodyguard to a very important part of your soul. It wanted to keep you safe because that value is part of your core essence. It being hurt or damaged–by being exposed to the world and rejected or ridiculed–would be and has been incredibly painful. After all, this isn't your office's or anyone else's mission which you can easily hide behind. This is your life purpose. And in order for you to achieve your highest purpose, you are required to offer it with humility.

I want you to know that I am so proud of you for even having the big brass ovaries or cojones to pick this book up. Most people live their lives with their heads in the sand, too scared to face their fears. But you are not hiding anymore. That is because you are clinging to your mustard seed of faith that there is more to life than survival mode. And that is all you need to move the mountains you're being called to upend in the world. I am so very proud of you, my friend.

Back to Imposter syndrome-crushing tools!

I have been the vehicle for some pretty insane outcomes. When I walk into the interview room, or the courtroom, or the operations command post, I am in flow. I am aware I move with confidence. My body language and posture let those around me that I know what I'm doing, and I do this instinctively. I get asked frequently how I was able to achieve so much. And although I generally prefer to live life as authentically and honestly as possible, what I realized some years ago was that I needed to do a better job of sharing the complete story of my "success." The truth is, it wasn't me at all. It was completely a God thing. And I'm not saying that in a platitude-y way. I'm being dead serious. Here's why.

For two to three days before every single operation I've ever done, my imposter rears its ugly head. I remember the first time I experienced its resurgence. It was about five minutes after I purchased the domain rights to my website. I was elated to have taken the leap one minute, and the next, I was in the fetal position on my couch. My gremlin was so loud in my mind. Intrusive thoughts asking me who I thought I was, that I would be ridiculed to pieces, and that my silly little website would accomplish nothing. It almost felt like something was clawing at my throat. For someone who has spent her life keeping up appearances that she has it all together, I was completely debilitated at that moment. I kept trying to rationalize what was happening to make it go away. I had felt so much joy only a few moments before. What the heck happened?

I now understand that my gremlin will always get loud when God is about to do something big in my life.** And so the pattern when I was leading statewide operations was two to three days of imposter syndrome overwhelm. It's first marked by crazy anxiety, ruminating thoughts, and mild depression, and I'm left bewildered as to where it came from. When I ask myself the following question, everything changes:

What am I experiencing in my body?

The answer eventually gets to identifying and acknowledging hopelessness.

Sadness, anger, frustration…I can handle all of these pretty well. But hopelessness? It's a black hole of life. Then I ask myself:

When else have I experienced this?

And then my memory banks get triggered.

Ah, yes. Literally EVERY time I'm about to do an operation.

It's the same nonsense dialogue. "This will never work. You're going to get all these people together, and nothing will happen. It'll be a waste of resources, and everyone is going to be so mad at you. They are sacrificing their weekends because of you. What if you get zero arrests and zero disclosures of live child victims who are being exploited? Everyone will know you're a POS, and your career will be over. They'll laugh you out of town."

And once again, my rational brain kicks my fight-or-flight reflex into high gear. My internal dialogue even consists of me negotiating with my gremlin.

"Ok, I think you're right. What if I cancel the operation? It's literally MY op, after all. I am the boss. They'll understand. I can totally do that!!"

Except that these operations take months to plan and involve fifty to one hundred agents, investigators, intel analysts, and support staff who are all geared up and excited. As I continue to acknowledge and get curious about my hopelessness, I arrive at another Truth: we've never had an op that wasn't successful. I'm not trying to squint and imagine results that don't exist just to make myself feel better. We have arrested multiple suspects, identified multiple live victims, and recovered multiple sexually exploited minors in every operation I've ever done. And the prosecution statistics are a matter of public record. What also stands out to me about this dialogue is that it reminds me of another thing:

I suffer from TERRIBLE spiritual amnesia.

Every time I'm about to stretch myself and create something no one else has, my imposter syndrome screams at me. I forget all about my past successes. I forget that the very first arrest we ever got on this one particular operation was a retired police officer. I forget that the many months of preparation and coordination were filled with naysayers, doubters, and even a couple of people who actively tried to stop the work from ever coming to light. I forget that we were victorious after an anonymous suspect engaged us in a three-hour surveillance detection game before we caught him. Only to discover he was a previously convicted sex offender. And oh, by the way, the subsequent investigation disclosed he had multiple additional live child victims. I forget about the serial rapist and the other dirty cops and coaches and all the tiny intuitive hits so many people got along the way that led us to achieve justice. In a profession where you will frequently hear things like, "Something told me to go look over here" which resulted in a major break in the investigation, it's easy to dismiss these tiny God moments in favor of purely rational thinking.

Most importantly, I forget what God has done for ME. God took little old me who fought him tooth and nail for a good chunk of my career. A reluctant Moses too, scared to simply obey what God was asking them to do.

"I don't want to be an agent."

"I don't want to go to HQ"

[Ok, I actually did want to deploy–I was still really pissed about the twin towers.]

"I don't want to lead the conversation with that senior Japanese government official."

"I definitely don't want to be a Pentagon bodyguard."

Remember the power of awareness. It is the most difficult and most powerful part of the process because once you're aware; you can choose a different thought or action. And now that I am aware and because I've done this enough times that I know what this cycle looks like for me, I do choose a different course of action.

Surrender.

"Alani, what the hell? Are you serious right now?"

Yes, friend. Yes, I am.

In a world filled with anger and victim mindset, our greatest weapons are spiritual ones. If you believe in the Christian teachings, all God requires us to do is bring our fish and loaves. They are not adequate for the task at hand. Not by a long shot. But if you offer them up to the Divine with humility and ask that God take them, He will do immeasurably more than you could have ever imagined.

This surrender looks different for everyone. For me, I have curated a process of stillness, meditation, time in the Bible, and a kick-ass playlist comprised of songs that speak what I feel even when I don't have the words. Skillet, Shinedown, Bad Wolves, System of a Down, Panic! At the Disco, and Papa Roach. Their lyrics are the vehicles I use to remind myself to:

"Shine a light in the dark,
let me see where you are,
'cause I'm not gonna leave you behind."

– Shinedown "Unity"

"Lord I want to feel your heart
And see the <u>world</u> through your eyes
I want to be your <u>hands</u> and feet
I want to live a life that leads

Ready yourselves
Ready yourselves
Let us <u>shine</u> the <u>light</u> of Jesus in the <u>darkest</u> night
Ready yourselves
Ready yourselves
May the <u>powers</u> of <u>darkness</u> tremble as our <u>praises</u> rise
Until the <u>whole</u> world <u>hears</u> Lord we are <u>calling</u> out
Lifting up Your name for all to hear the sound
Like <u>voices</u> in the <u>wilderness,</u> we're <u>crying</u> out
As the day <u>draws</u> near
We'll sing <u>until</u> the <u>whole</u> world hears

Lord let your <u>sleeping</u> giant arise
Catch the <u>demons</u> by surprise
Holy <u>nation</u> sanctified
Let this be our <u>battle</u> cry

Want to be your <u>hands</u> and feet
Want to be a life that leads
To see you set the <u>captive</u> free
Until the <u>whole</u> world hears
And I pray that they will see more of you and less of me
Lord I want my life to be the song You sing
Until the <u>whole</u> world <u>hears</u> Lord we are <u>calling</u> out"
     – Casting Crowns "Until the Whole World Hears"

It's a process I use when I feel completely weak and useless. But that is exactly where the magic happens. Remember that in God's economy, he uses weak vessels to manifest His greatest strength.

1 Cor 12:22 "The parts of the body that seem to be weaker are indispensable."

2 Cor 12:9-10 "But He said to me, 'My grace is sufficient you, for my power is made perfect in weakness.' Therefore I will boast all the more gladly about my weaknesses, so that Christ's power may rest in me. That is why, for Christ's sake, I delight in weaknesses, in insults, in hardships, in persecutions, in difficulties. For when I am weak, then I am strong."

Psa 73: 26 "My flesh and my heart may fail, but God is the strength of my heart and my portion forever."

Isa 40:29 "He gives strength to the weary and increases the power of the weak."

Matt 11:28 "Come to me, all you who are weary and burdened, and I will give you rest."

Rom 8:26 "In the same way, the Spirit helps us in our weakness. We do not know what we ought to pray for, but the Spirit himself intercedes for us through wordless groans."

Phi 4:13 "I can do all things through him who gives me strength."

2 Tim 1:7 "For the spirit God gave us does not make us timid, but gives us power, love, and self-discipline."

And so, I embrace my weakness. And at some point over these two or three days of suffering and spiritual battle, something happens. I can't describe it, but I just go. A flip gets switched, and I'm doing the work. It's not work at all; it's a state of being. And before I know it, it's done. The results are astounding…again. And I can't claim credit for any of it.

A brief word on defining success. The world defines it as titles, awards, money, and power. When I arrived at the proverbial top of my field long before these flow states, I looked around and realized I didn't feel fulfilled. I discovered it was because I had supplanted my values with the world's. On my journey to this flow state, I decided I would never again do my heart's work and not take a moment to be present.

And so now I do. Every operation, even though I'm juggling command post communications with the field, intelligence analysts providing awesome raw data, agents making notifications, agency leaders to keep informed, and all the stress that comes with it, I will always very intentionally pause for a period of two to three minutes and look around. I become present. It's usually around the zero dark thirty lulls. I observe my tired but alert partners working away. I take in the walls filled with communications and safety plans, information, targets, and recoveries. I see the tokens left next to workstations–an investigator's favorite candy, a reminder of an inside joke, a totem, or a printed meme intended to distract them from the difficulty of fighting evil. I hear the chatter over the radio and remember there are 30+ people in the field volunteering to do the exciting but also dangerous work of surveilling and apprehending the perpetrators.

And then I remember that they are there because of me.

Periodically, I get messages from them.

At 2 am. "We're not quitting until you tell us we're done, Alani."

Over text message. "Thank you for reminding me why I joined law enforcement."

After the debriefing. "This is the purest work I have ever done."

After a particularly tough surveillance and arrest operation where the suspect utilized some pretty advanced countersurveillance techniques, the command post erupted in cheers as the communication came over the radio that the suspect was in custody. I keyed the mic on the radio, so the arrest and surveillance teams could hear the jubilation.

The arrest team leader later confided that hearing those cheers lifted his exhausted spirit, and it would be a moment he would never forget. And because he had the vulnerability to share how much that moment meant to him, I will also never forget that moment and that conversation.

And I had a new definitely of success and fulfillment: authentic connection. To the mission, to my fellow justice seekers, and to myself.

All because of a crazy vision I had that only a few people bought off on at first. That operation now spans oceans and continues to yield fruit even though I am long gone. And I am completely humbled at this incredible and brilliant group of humans I have the privilege to sharpen and who sharpen me.

Who am I to be so favored to be in this position?

And so, I now know that my imposter points me to my greatest gifts and successes. And every time I feel the hopelessness in my gut and want to throw up, and I ask myself, when else I've experienced this, and I come to the awareness that I've experienced this before…

…I now smirk.

Because I know something amazing is about to happen.

CHAPTER 10

Fail Faster

Not every client's process of harnessing their gremlin looks exactly like mine. What is most important for you to understand is that it is a process to get to an understanding of what yours looks like. You may try it the first time, and it may not go as I described above. It will feel very messy and confusing, and you may even feel like a failure. Or it's even possible the objective which you sought to achieve doesn't result in a "mission accomplished." Your Imposter syndrome will tell you that you're not doing the process properly. As if there were only one way of doing it right! Reframe it into an opportunity to learn with the goal to fail faster. The faster and more often you try, the more feedback you're going to receive. Remembering that thoughts → feelings → behaviors and that we know we are on the right path when we feel the fruits of the spirit (ie: love, joy, peace, patience, etc):

How do you feel about how this test went?

What behaviors did you engage in that you feel really great about?

What areas provide opportunities for growth and a greater understanding of what your imposter syndrome cycle looks like?

What will you do differently next time?

Utilize your support network, a therapist, counselor, or coach to help you dig into the experience to uncover those a-ha moments. And remember that it takes a lot of energy and work to burn old mindsets and belief structures to the ground and build new more life-giving ones in their place. Showing yourself grace or allowing others to speak empowering words to you when you can't do it for yourself, is another imposter syndrome-busting tool. It is hard to ask for help. If you're struggling with this, I want you to imagine your best friend or co-worker. If they came to you and asked for what you needed, would you judge them? Absolutely not. The giving and supportive person you are would jump into action mode and help fill the void. Imagine how great it feels to be able to support your network to achieving their highest potential. Feels amazing, right?

Now what are you robbing your support network of by not asking for help?

What are you robbing yourself of by avoiding asking for the same support you would freely give to anyone?

CHAPTER 11

The Least of Us

Three hours after my 'terp and I had left the forward operating base (FOB), my boss called me. "Where are you?"

I was just about done debriefing my informant on a pending suicide vest (SVEST) attack on US service members. Three locals had been manipulated into putting the deadly vests on and the attack was projected to happen later that evening. As I passed the geographical coordinates of where the house lodging the attackers was, I noted the silence on the other end of the phone as my boss finished writing them down. "Good job. I'm going to pass this on to the [special operations] teams for action, but we'll talk about this when you get back."

The silence was heavy in the Hilux as my 'terp and I made our way to base. I thought we'd done the right thing, but the doubts had produced a serious knot in my stomach. What if I got sent home? It was not uncommon for people to get kicked off missions and out of the country if you weren't up-to-snuff. I didn't want to embarrass my agency and home office by having to explain why I didn't complete the entire deployment. But I knew in my bones that we had made the right decision even if my boss disagreed.

As I entered the plywood SCIF (a room that processes classified information) and walked into my boss's office, he looked up from his computer and told me the operators had been successful in thwarting the attack…and that if I ever pulled such a stunt again without authorization, I would be sent home.

The senior intel analyst working on that portfolio later pulled me aside and said I was the first agent in over three years to get a new source (aka informant) on the books.

Do I know how many lives were saved – if any – that day? No. And I won't while I'm still on this side of heaven.

Will you – the human resources employee–know the full impact of you catching a pay error and fixing it without telling anyone? No. Because of your actions, an employee was paid on time which perhaps meant they were able to avoid eviction or foreclosure. Or maybe they didn't have to rely on their credit card whose interest rate would snowball and cripple them over time.

Will you – the psychotherapist – know the full impact of a session where a client seemed very resistant to your tools and techniques? No. Because maybe that rumble planted a seed that doesn't bear fruit for years and certainly long after they've stopped coming to your practice.

Will you–the trafficking investigator – understand how effective you were after the 5th, 10th, and 50th time a trafficking victim goes back to their trafficker or their drug of choice? After all the blood, sweat, and tears you put into the case? No. But I have many emails and notes from survivors notifying us that – because of a sting operation a decade ago where they were recovered – they are now living a sober life, have a beautiful family, and have steady employment. And that survivor never gave any indication at the time of recovery that they desperately wanted out of their circumstances. And the truth is, most of the time we can't find that investigator, because they've retired or we don't have a complete name to go off of.

If you receive feedback on the incredible impact of your actions, consider it a massive blessing.

But in the meantime, trust that your work is having ripple effects in the world that you will never fully see or understand in this lifetime.

[37] "Then the righteous will answer him, 'Lord, when did we see you hungry and feed you, or thirsty and give you something to drink? [38] When did we see you a stranger and invite you in, or needing clothes and clothe you? [39] When did we see you sick or in prison and go to visit you?'

[40] "The King will reply, 'Truly I tell you, whatever you did for one of *the least of these* brothers and sisters of mine, you did for me.' – Matthew 25:37-40 NIV

The key to unlocking this level of influence and impact is hidden at the center of your imposter syndrome. And you know that awareness is the single most powerful step you can take to unleashing your greatest potential. Where being the "least" in service of the least of us makes you the most powerful tool.

See you on the battlefield.

We have already won the war.

www.ingramcontent.com/pod-product-compliance
Lightning Source LLC
Chambersburg PA
CBHW050756160726
48004CB00002B/579